RAINDROPS TO WATERFALLS

My Life Poetry

Michael Van Pelt

Outskirts Press, Inc.
Denver, Colorado

The opinions expressed in this manuscript are solely the opinions of the author and do not represent the opinions or thoughts of the publisher. The author represents and warrants that s/he either owns or has the legal right to publish all material in this book. If you believe this to be incorrect, contact the publisher through its website at www.outskirtspress.com.

Raindrops To Waterfalls
My Life Poetry
All Rights Reserved
Copyright © 2006 Michael Van Pelt

This book may not be reproduced, transmitted, or stored in whole or in part by any means, including graphic, electronic, or mechanical without the express written consent of the publisher except in the case of brief quotations embodied in critical articles and reviews.

Outskirts Press
http://www.outskirtspress.com

ISBN-10: 1-59800-464-6
ISBN-13: 978-1-59800-464-9

Outskirts Press and the "OP" logo are trademarks belonging to
Outskirts Press, Inc.

Printed in the United States of America

DEDICATED TO

George & Rosie Jones

And

Izayah Van-Pelt

Table of Contents

Acknowledgements I
Special Thanks III
From The Editor V
Introduction VII

1 .... When a Raindrop Falls
2 .... I Imagine
3 .... Eyes That Met
4 .... One
5 .... In Dreams
6 .... Celibacy
7 .... What Women Want
8 .... Loving You
9 .... The Secret Ring
10 .... Rumors
11 .... Worries
12 .... To-get-her
13 .... A Lesser Man
15 .... Cheating Hearts
16 .... Questionable Thoughts
17 .... Bag Lady

18	God Tears
19	Hidden Fist
20	Tinted Eyes
21	A Bitter-less Woman
22	Awaken
23	Catch Me
24	A Dying You
25	Beauty
26	Dear Heartache
27	Cupid
28	Rain
29	You're Smile
30	This Old House
31	Childhood
32	Declining
33	Unwanted Weed
34	Faith
35	A Woman's Test
36	Runaway Child
37	Wondering
38	You Remind Me
39	Thoughts of Loving You
40	D.E.P.R.E.S.S.I.O.N.
41	Words UN-plain
42	ME?
43	You and Me
44	LIKE
45	A Lonely Child
46	FALLEN
47	Constantly
48	Good News
49	Tears from the Past
50	Some Say
51	All Alone
52	Feel like going home
53	Even if
54	Understanding
55	My unborn Child

56	The Messenger
57	Confused
58	Someday I will Pray
59	If I
60	I See
61	Shut Eyes
62	Losing you
63	If I (2)
64	Death
65	Friendship
66	The Angel
67	When a Man Cries
68	The Third Person
69	Forbidden
70	I Miss You
71	Unfaithful
72	Blinded
73	My Mama
74	Me & Money'
75	Mistakes
76	The Shielded Truth
77	Love Hung-over
78	The Truth
79	Footsteps
80	Runaway
81	A battle for Love
82	Fatherhood
83	The Last Day of Last Words
84	For the sake of You
85	Just Believe
86	Trading Love
87	Us
88	Born Again
89	Betrayed
90	Growing Young
91	Judging Me
92	Familiar
93	Raindrops to Waterfalls

Acknowledgements

Though this book required my life experiences and trials, I was never alone as I thought. So forth, I would like to thank the Lord Jesus Christ because without him I wouldn't have been blessed with the gift of writing, my family; Melvin Clay, Tina Parker, James Van-Pelt, Curtis Van-Pelt, Kim Van-Pelt, Lisa Van-Pelt, George Jones III and my son, Izayah Van-Pelt

And last, but certainly not least my mother Ms. Rosie Jones

God Bless

Special Thanks to My Supporters

Thanks to my editor Zette Washington, for the long months and hours of hard work. To Tomeka Davis, for her patience and support, and to the Forest Barber Shop located in Little Rock, AR. for my first book signing.

From the Editor

It has been a pleasure working with Michael and assisting him with fulfilling his dream.

I pray that all who read these poems will be touched enlightened and gain a new perspective in their own lives.

These poems will take you back to your childhood, through adolescence, into adulthood.

ENJOY!

Zette Washington

Introduction

    This is a chronicle of my true life experiences, with love and life itself. My thoughts and feelings, as I remembered. Although this book is of no order of occurrences it is all true. Here too, are my personal exchanges with society. My knowledge of opinions are not withheld, but shared and my recollection of articulated ideas and words as written in very specific phrases in their contents.
    My memories seem quite distant, but its reality keeps them revised.
    Nevertheless I have to be faithful to both fact and feeling. And to this world my book Raindrops to Waterfalls was born, revealing the true poetic quotes of my young minded experiences with life's ups and downs creating my poetic circle.
    I never imagined myself as much of a writer, but yet my life became a story. My regrets of selfish acts of carelessness of my emotions and judgmental heart became the downfall of my very own feelings. And as a child, my writings were still yet young, never knowing what plans life had for me, but the message was received.

Now my mind is refreshed and for the ones I've touched in negative ways, please forgive my actions of neglects, for its routine is no more of my tranquility and my soulful mind can now rest.

RAINDROPS TO WATERFALLS

My Life Poetry

When a Raindrop Falls

When a rain drop falls
They say a seed
Is formed
And when a seed
Is formed a child
Is born
And when a child is born
Then love is reformed
And when love is reformed
The earth no longer mourns
And when the earth no
Longer mourns
It sets off inner
Alarms
And after the inner
Alarms
Then hate is warned
After hate is warned
Then the brighter
The sun
And the brighter the sun
Then you know that love
Has won

I IMAGINE

I can imagine snow
In mid July
And I can imagine rain
That falls up from the ground
Instead of the sky
But it's hard to imagine
Me without you
From the first day
To the last day
I knew you'd
Come to stay
Making all my
Cloudy days somehow
Fade away
The trauma you nearly
Caused when you went
Astray and in all my life
I never dreamed of this day
And the tears
Warmed my eyes
And blur by vision and
Showered the earth
Giving my heart every reason
For every breath I breathe
It's not only for one
But two
And for every step I take
Hopefully
It will bring me
Closer to you.

EYES that MET

Only once did I see her
It was only a glance
Our eyes met for one second
Spoiling my chance
Again they met,
My feet being swept
Catching my breath and
My heart she kept
Leaving me nothing
But her image behind
Going back to the same place hoping
To find
Some sort of clue of whom
She really was
Mad at myself just because,
Was I too shy or just afraid?
Thinking what a beautiful
Couple we would have made
Good things come and go
But I feel this one is gone
Walking by the same place hoping
She's at home..........

ONE

One smile
One cry
One laugh
One lie
One step
One door
One tear
One floor
One hand
One man
One woman
One day
One night
One way
One fight
One he
One she
One stay
One flee
One world
One ME.....?

IN DREAMS

We all have dreams
When we are asleep
But no matter how
Hard we hold on
Dreams we can
Never keep with us
As we're awakened
Trying to bring back
What we have found
But still they're taken
How can we lose?
Something we never had
At that time something
So real
But not real enough
To hold within our hands
Reaching for the stars
That fall
From the sky
Grabbing for their brightness
But only reaching
Them with our eyes
Hoping to save something
For tomorrow
But dreams are not ours to keep
Only to borrow
When you dream
Dream all you can
Because they're your dreams
And they're only
For you to
Understand

CELIBACY

Let me educate YOU
About your inexperienced
Mind
Robbing you of your emotions
And making them mine
Foolish child, if only you knew
Child
Taking your anger
And stuffing it into
A barrel of happiness and smiles,
You're not incapable
Of determining the love
Of Life
I worship you and only you
Hampering your love for the truth
My controllable sexuality
Of our every meeting
This is something not so easy
But marvelously
I'm stripping your mind of the
Non relating negativity
Punishing your body
With positive notions
Transforming your
Mind in the shape of an ocean
Destroying the walls
In which you built
But yet respecting your morals
Of Celibacy

What Women Want

No whispers
No fainted cries
No bad hellos
No sad good-byes
No Faraway footsteps
No letters left
While she slept
No dry kisses
No new misses
Only the arms to shield
Her from the cold
To hold forever together
Until you grow old

LOVING YOU

Love is like a river that
Flows into the sea
Spreading things apart once
Like you and me
When will love misery cease
Blameless as why the mocking bird
Really sings
While the beating of my heart
And why is loving you still a mystery
With our thoughts linked between
Our memories

L is for the **love** you bring
O is for the **offering**
V is for the **victory**
E is for the satisfying **everything**

Loving you is really easy
Losing you would be displeasing

Y is for **you** and me
O is for **opportunity**
U is for **understanding**

Loving you.... why is it so demanding.....?

The Secret Ring

The secrets it holds
Once placed on the finger
It goes where you go
It knows what you know
Holding the stories yet to be told
Traveling to different places
Left aboard in hands of different faces
It agrees to whatever you agree
And never tells whatever it sees
Subdued in silence and shame
Vowed never to reveal any names
The look of harshness
The look of pain
With watchful eyes and
Who's to blame.................?

RUMORS

Gentle whispers that has
Come to past,
Relationships starting up
But knowingly that they
Will not last,
Hello does it really
Mean goodbye?
Prepare yourself to
Dry your teary
Eyes,
I know that love
Comes and goes,
I heard a rumor
So tell me if
You know,
Are you keeping
Secrets deep down
Below?
Tell me if you
Have the answer
Before you go,
Rumors that fall like
The snow,
If you're leaving surely
I would like to know

WORRIES

I'm sorry if I couldn't
Cure your worried mind
Your hidden thoughts
I could not find
Leaving me puzzled
And confined
Thinking how could
I be so blind
Still searching and still I
Could not find
All the worries that's
On your mind

TOGETHER
(to-get-her)

I never thought
That I would
Have to let you go
But I couldn't continue
To go through this
Anymore
And for that short time
That we were together
I treated each day
Like it was
Forever
How un-clever was I
Not to realize
The real reasons why
We were no longer
Together
When we met
It was you and I
Together
Facing each others problems
Trying to solve them
But one couldn't
I believe that together
That there was nothing
We couldn't do
Or go through
Together
You and me against the world
Together
To Get Her
To   Get   Her
For-Ever

A Lesser? Man

Just because a man cry
Doesn't make him a
Lesser man,
You just don't understand
Just because some men don't
Beat you and curse you……..
But when some men try
To love you
Why do you laugh
At them?
Some men are not of a weaker
Breed,
Making Love instead of
Having casual sex
Fulfilling your needs
Doesn't make him a

Lesser man,

We're only human
Believe it or not
Pushing us away
But we'll never stop
wanting you
If you see some men cry
It's not because of pain,
It's because they are
A Real Man,
We're your salvation
When you're weary
And sad,
Now do you think
That's still a
Lesser Man?

Our fragile touches
Melts your hearts
Holding you tightly
Bringing back your
Feelings of love
Making you love
Again,
Now tell me
Are these words
Of
Lesser Man

CHEATING HEARTS

How do you help
A cheating heart?
If it never complains,
Destroying lives
And nothings ever
The same,
Taking away what
Love once made
The feelings of guilt
Once you've misbehaved,
But cheating hearts
Are lonely hearts
That has lost its way
So by letting them go
Will make for better days,
Every once in a while
You'll come across a cheating heart
Just point them in another direction
And let them find their own way through
The Dark

QUESTIONABLE THOUGHTS

I thought I needed
You,
Just because I was alone
Facing each day alone
I thought I needed
Your kisses
I thought I needed
You to hold me

But I didn't

I thought I needed
Your comfort
Your advice and your love

But I didn't

All this time I thought
I needed you

But all along

All I needed was

ME

To Love

ME

BAG-LADY

You may never see her cry
And she may never speak
Whenever you walk by
But if you could read her eyes
You can try to guess why
Her hidden secrets of mistrust and lies
And to her surprise
Her eyebrow rises
And she sometimes lets out silent sighs
And she tries to hold on for happier days
Often taking life's lonely stroll
Down life's lonely road
Her thoughts running out of control
But finds the strength to carry the heavy load

GOD'S TEARS

Every time I close my
Eyes it's as if I'm
Hearing fainting
Cries and I'm
Remembering those big
Brown eyes
So fragile your tears
Of remembered love
Barricading my mind
Of the unwanted
Truth about life
We are **One**
Only beneath the only
One
Who truly loves
Everyone
Sometimes even the
Earth gives into
The rain and
Soaks it in
Willing as if it's
Opening its heart
Nobody knows pain
Like that one day
I didn't see you
Smiling, but crying
So deep inside
And for that
Short moment
I knew

HIDDEN FIST

How can you see footprints
Within the wind?
With no traces of others
Hidden sins,
Befriended at the end
Of each path
No control of ones careless
Soul
And who will ever know,
(your secret)
What of those forgetful
Cheers,
The laugh less years
No more warmed tears
The painless pain,
The touch less shame
And what is your real name,
Is it tomorrow, or is
It yesterday?
No need to touch or curl
No need to neither run nor vanish
Your thoughts within your mind
How can you see bruises
That's not so kind to
The naked eye?
They're only to be heard

TINTED EYES

Shallow words often
Means shallow thoughts
And long days often
Mean long walks
Who am I to judge?
The shifting of your eye's
The turn of your head
The before and after
Lies, so watchful through
These tinted eyes
My words may not be enough
To move your feet
Unanswered good-byes
The sleepless weeks
Choosing each word carefully
Whenever I speak
Through these tinted eyes
In days often making me weak

A Bitter-less Woman

Bitter words from a bitter mind
Bitter taste from a sweet wine
Whom to hear these bitter cries
From a dry mouth and bitter eyes
If looks could kill, you would soon die
No need for questions, with answers of
Bitter lies
Engraved in her hands, stitched in her
Soul
The bitter sound of love echoing
From all around
Do not touch the face with a bitter frown
Taunted like the unfunny clown
How can one say things of bitterness
Hopelessness and carelessness
To the mother of the earth,
The breath from her lungs
Useless to breathe of what you deny
A woman's bitter life
A long ride,
A long journey,
Still sitting waiting for love to arrive.

AWAKEN

Listen and tell me if you
Can hear,
The sound of crowded thoughts
With no room for fear
A bitter taste forms in my mouth
Whenever someone comes near
The days may pass
But who is still left here
With blackened eyes and sore feet
Spending too much running and
To weak to speak
I called out last night
For I was trapped in a dream
While hearing laughter and
Who could be so mean ?
And everywhere I saw footprints
In which someone once stood
A cloudy night of dreams and
Of what I'm still unsure

CATCH ME
(For Izayah)

Catch me if you can with your fragile
Hands
I know you're not yet a man
But one day you'll understand
It's not my fault I was there
Standing in the shadows of your tears
I watched you grow for years within
My mind,
And over time I fell behind
And I have nothing to remind me of you
No vision of your first lost tooth
And you ask where was who
Past lies have left you confused
Running through doorways
Looking for clues
Catch me if you can,
Here is where I stand
Take my invisible hand
Whenever you should grow
There's one thing you should know
That there is no you without me…., genetically
So catch one last thing
And hold throughout our life ending
And that's my

L.O.V.E.

A Dying You

When it's cold outside and the wind blows
Sometimes I can hear whispers
And its words cut through my soul
Like a knife through flesh
Chanting out the bitterness of losing
Your smile
Reacting to the bitterness of forgive-less-ness
I wish I had a thousand chances
To save you, to save us from drifting apart
Like night and day we were once one
Like leaves on a tree
That falls to the cold ground in winter
And what was it like breathing
On your own for the first time
Unlike your first steps and unlike your first cry
So close your eyes and flyaway with me
Until tomorrow appears without questions
Of yesterday with words untouched
Blink once and it's gone never
To appear again
Forgotten as if you've
Forgotten me

BEAUTY

I love beauty unfaithfully
While standing next to deaden trees
Empty rivers and flightless honeybees
Blue less skies and desert lands
Towering mountain tops with no
Running streams
Dirty rain and quiet stormy seas
Children not laughing but
Standing on crumbled leaves
The wind never blows and
Snowfalls are never cold
Everything is old and Dixie still sings
No highways or byways when nothing
Ever goes your way
No starry nights
Just a darkened moon
No early morning sunshine
Just misery and gloom
Where is beauty
How far has she roamed?
Never to see her again
Forever left in a world
To grow ugly alone

Dear HEARTACHE

Dear heartache,
I'm sorry but I have
Some bad news,
It is you who will now
Receive your own blues,
I have no use for you anymore
So pack your bags and
Take your pain out
The door,
Because the love of my life
Has returned
Now the feelings are back
And your misery
I know longer yearn,
I know this is hard for you
Because you're use to having
Me around,
But no longer are you
Wanted because love is what I've found,
So good-bye heartache
You won't be missed
Because you're the last
Problem off my list

CUPID

I blame Cupid for all my problems
He thought his arrows could somehow
Solve them
Filling my heart with joy
Bringing together a girl
And a boy
But Cupid missed his mark
Bringing back the void
Of loneliness, going
From ending back to start
If only I hadn't seen him
That day
I wonder would I be
Feeling this way
Instead of helping me
He just sealed my hearts fate
Because Cupid knows nothing
About love

RAIN

Rain, why must you call
My name
The sins from my tears
Causes me pain
And nothing is ever
The same
Shouting out your name
In vain
And still I can't
Complain
It brings me down and
Everyday is the same
But only when
It rains
The ocean, the waves and the trees
If it wasn't for you
Where would they be?
Hiding in the shadows
Like me

Your Smile

Some men will love you
For your body
But I will love you only
For your smile
Just the other day
I saw you smile
A bright ray of sunshine, that
Seemed to gleam my way
Nobody knows the things
Your smile can do
Or undo
Bad things that will turn wise men
Into fools
If ever a smile
As lively as yours…..
There would be no winner
Only an even score
The things your smile can do
The changes your smile
Puts one through…….

This OLD HOUSE

Early in the morning, before the sunrise
I sit by my bedroom window
All sleepy-eyed
And my mind feels somewhat at ease,
Yawning as the coming of the daylight
Breeze and I can hear the
Rustling of the fall leaves
In this old house
And the calling of the tamed wild
The cries of a yearling child
Bring forth the noise of life
In this old house
The TV's playing your favorite show
While witnessing the first falling of the winter snow
              In this old house.

CHILDHOOD

A baby's first cry is more songful
Than any birds melody
And their smile is more sight-full
Than the first day of spring
And their eyes filled with tears
As if like an ocean
Safe from hate,
Protected by love
With open arms in motion
Their first words are beautiful
And their first steps are taken
Very carefully
While sleeping peacefully
And in their dreams
How can they do harm
Trapped deep in sleep
In their mothers loving arms
And each day to them is still the same
Responding to their familiar name
Constantly having growing pains,
But all would be worth it if we
Could go back to our
Childhood
Again

Declining

If I should fall
Will you catch me?
And if I should lose my way
Will you tell me how to find it?
If I should cry
Will you dry my eyes?
And if I should hear lies
Will you tell me the truth?
If I should ever become fearful of the world
Will you shield me from its pain?
And if I should ever stray……, and return
Will your feelings still be the same……………

UNWANTED WEED

It grows amongst the rose that bloom
Looking jealously through a window
Into an empty room
Almost never wanted nor needed
It waits, hoping and pleading often,
Asking the rose to trade places
Crying deep down inside
Knowing its words are true
Making the rose feel guilty and blue
They both breathe the same air and
Drink the same water
And when the time comes, the rose is
Gently picked and placed inside the house
In a beautiful vase leaving the weed to later
Be sprayed or cut
And the moral is (everything must change, nothing ever
remains the same)
Except for the rain and the clouds
Never to realize the true beauty
Is at the roots
Never judge anything before looking
Deep within

FAITH

How can I be free
When there's days I can't even sleep
How can life rob me of my fruitful leaves,
with snow bound grounds and
My last breath,
gone with one squeeze
And yet there's no relief
Stricken with faith
And whom do we seek
Lost in the night
Like lost shepherd sheep
The coming of darkness
Over day it creeps

A Woman's Test

A woman's test of love and innocence
Is just a trail of bad remembrance
Of how love fell, trap so deep as if
In a well
And a story some must tell
How dare thee denounce me as if
I was never there
A child born of love and hate
And his life you tried to take
Luckily God held on to his grace
And the look on his face
When he came to be
A product of you and me
Separated by fate,
If only I waited
A woman's test of lies and betrayal
Like a runaway train your life
Derailed.

Runaway Child

Can you hear the raindrops
Falling to the ground,
Trapped in a world of unwanted frowns,
Can you feel the wind blowing
Within your mind,
Blowing for dear life and
Still cannot find,
Hopefully one day it will come
Those three words that you still hum,
Who smiles a needless smile,
Who screams within a crowded crowd,
When laughter never touches your lips,
No hardened hands to
Grasp your hips,
Hiding your feelings within
The shadows that seals your doom,
You're like a runaway child
That only runs to
Their room

Wondering

Your eyes tell me that you've been
Seeing lies
Betrayed like the slaves
With shifted eyes
Looking over your shoulder
Whenever I walk by
I wonder what you're thinking
Expressing myself with sighs
Looking at me with unholy eyes
Not saying anything to my surprise
But up-rise, standing on two feet
Faced with reality, until we meet
Not knowing your thoughts
Sometimes scares me
Watching you while your expression flees
Watching your lips, yet no one speaks
Unless spoken to
No where to turn, nothing to lose
Sitting, not standing at last we meet
Touching, holding, putting my
Wondering thoughts to sleep

You Remind Me

Your lips remind me of yesterday
The innocence of a young heart
Playful emotions of tearless dreams
With visions of whatever may seem
Your eyes remind me of the stars
In the sky

Two puddles of waterfall
That's destined to rise
Your skin reminds me of silk
The rareness of its form
And your love reminds me of
The burning sun

The Thoughts of LOVING YOU

Heaven will be calling soon,
Because an angel is missing
And I think it's you,
Entering a life without gloom
And I shall continue
To quote my philosophy
About loving you,
My evidence is your truth
To deny us would be cruel
Born into a world of undisciplined feelings,
Unanswered mistakes,
Revealing life's true identity of
Integrating your untouched beauty,
But how can love survive individually
Without the thought of you and me
Successfully uniting
Uplifting the thoughts of loving

D.E.P.R.E.S.S.I.O.N.

Deep in sleep
Everything is fine, as night and day,
Pretending like the sun will never shine again,
Remembering only the rain
Everything is fine, as the first day of spring
Suspended in time, awaiting what tomorrow may bring,
Silently whispering
Inside
Only to awake,
Never to smile again.

"Words UN-plain"

The last time I saw you
You were standing in a puddle of borrowed tears,
Whose smile that somehow disappeared,
It was a treaty between the clouds,
Forming raindrops that would fall for years,
So previous the memory of forgotten peers,
Who are we to judge the world?
When the world no longer can breathe your name
And all the time it complains,
Putting its heart to strain and
Still no pain, but the stress
Still remains and what of its fame
Hidden between the words I and you,
Because some words don't come
Out too plain

ME?

I loved you more than I loved me
Not seeing the innocence of
An inner being pleading.
How could I forget about me?
When I'm remembering you,
I'm remembering nothing of thee
In actuality I used to adore me,
But never was I expecting me to leave.
Then all I had was you pretending
To look for me, where was I hiding?
In the shadows of dreams,
Waiting to be free,
But never tried escaping from
A prison of beauty,
Dedicated to the one who never loved me
And day by day I drifted far away
Planning to stay as we grew nearer and nearer,
But all was changed when I stood
In front of a broken mirror.

You and Me

When you cry, I cry
When you laugh, I laugh
And when you went away, I wasn't sad
Because I still kept our memory
Deep inside of me, gladly
I chose not to be sad,
When I can see you whenever I want
Inside my mind and I'll never be
Too far behind, running never walking,
Listening never talking
Because I know soon you'll return
To show me all the new things you've
Learned and we can start all over again
You and **M**e
Sitting together crying……

For Izayah

"LIKE"

Like a rose to a bush
I can feel your leaves covering me
Like April showers that seem to fall for hours
I feel ready for anything that life may bring,
Thinking should I risk it all,
Knowing that summer will soon turn into fall
Finally my dreams can cease
Clearing my mind
And for the first time,
I can think.

A Lonely Child

A lonely child sits in a crowded crowd,
Reaching within for deeper smiles
Then up springs the joy upon your entering,
Yet their fears surrendering to the love you bring
Uniting broken dreams and frozen tears,
Collected throughout the years
Freeing unanswered cries
No more teary eyes,
No more sad good-byes
Because no more shall you pass them by
Never again to encounter lies
For the past is gone and
No more are they alone
Because love brought you home

FALLEN

How do you wonder when my
Words are of stutter,
Memories that fade and then they become
And when you smile, my heart obeys
Every word you come to say
I've been waiting for so long without you
And now my arms can come to rest
No more **Fallen** dreams, for
I am now in peace,
And **For** the first time I can't cry
You are reprised
I've heard better things from
A laugh of beauty,
Fallen frowns to a cold hearted ground,
For the wind blows no more,
You are everything
Who could ask lesser to adore?
Why, when, will it ever not end, for
I've fallen for you.

Constantly

Constantly I hear
The sound from a voice
Through the walls of a shallow well
And if I answer
You'll think I'm crazy
So how can I ignore
The sounds of a calling
Constantly getting louder
As I sleep deeply

Good News

No news from the blues today
Now I can go out and play
For yesterday's gone and for it
I'm thankful
(Dear Lord, I'm very thankful)
I can better hear singing
From far away
Blue streams, once gray,
For I have good news today,
No more wondering through
Forests unknown, when to never walk
Alone, my speech forever toned
Now that I have good news,
My journey is now for home

Tears for the Past

Catch me now, if you dare
For I run along open shores
No more shall you chase me
Through open doors
Full of brightness and energy
Best friends is what we used to be
Now that we are enemies,
And the battle will never cease
Until you feel relief
And free from grief and
You may never find peace,
But still you're in none-belief
Unfaithful to you, no not quite
We were never a couple
Despite when we fuss and fight
Yes, I'm still running for your
Breath will not last
I'm here for the future and
Your tears for the past!

Some Say

Some say that love is
A misunderstanding between two fools
A lack of self respect
That's far from cool
Chasing memories that's long gone
Turning corners in your mind,
Leading you far from home

Some say if you love someone,
Let them go and if they return, let them stay
But if love was all that,
Then why in the first place they went away
Catching up to yesterday's news
Finding them gone, leaving you blue and confused

Some say in the end, you'll lose
Bringing to fact that love is only
A misunderstanding between two fools

All alone

All alone, there's nobody here, but me
Even my shadow abandons,
To know who you are is to be free
Alone, searching for peace
None existing, but here I be
So long Mr. Sunshine, hello rainy day
I can hear you falling, but you're much too late
I don't care if you come, so you might as well leave
Take away my heart and leave the pain
Please!
Alone am I, but do not cry
Sadness is among me, but no tears fall
From my eyes
Good-bye flowers, hello cool breeze

All alone in this world

Nobody's here but me

feel like going home

I know sometimes we all get tired
And feel like going home
I know a place not far from
Where you used to roam
It's a place where we all gather
A place we all can belong
A place of no suffering,
A place filled with songs
But if you ever get lonely and
You feel like going home
Just remember the good times
And hopefully it will make you strong
But if anyone should go before you
There's one thing you should know
That if an when you're ready to take
That long journey home
That God will be waiting to lead you down that road
Because if one go, we all go

Because no one walks alone

But only if you feel like going home

Even if

Even if it doesn't shine
Doesn't mean it's not worth a dime

Even if it doesn't snow
Doesn't mean you don't get cold

Even if I never see you cry
Doesn't mean you don't have tears in your eyes

Even if I'm not around
Doesn't mean I can't be found

Even if the words are not there
Doesn't mean I don't care

Even if you never thought I knew
Doesn't mean my mind's not on you

Even if you should go away
Doesn't mean I won't beg you to stay

Even if.............

UNDERSTANDING

I understand that you're leaving
Unlike bargaining, there's no pleading
Believing in miracles that will never exist
Forget-me-nots, unfinished lists
Everybody needs somebody to love

I understand you leaving
When push comes to shove
No love lost, no matter the cost

I understand nothing, but defeat
Only that I see there's no you
If there's no me

Understanding, nor demanding
Actuality, remembering everything
Which in reality is really

MISUNDERSTANDING

My Unborn Child

I can remember when she first told me
My puzzled mind was my reaction
Thinking how could this be

Mixed feelings and lost emotions for her honesty
Thinking what shall I do?
How can I raise this unborn child?
Young hearted and confused
What will her family think?
When she already has two

An agreement was made not to tell
Putting my unborn child through
What would soon be hell
Deep dwelled inside of her womb

A phone call was made and a
Doctor we will be visiting soon
Two Hundred dollars in my hand
And awaiting was an empty room

Five minutes later it was over
Just that quick
My feelings of guilt and to my stomach
I felt sick

How could I have been so selfish?
I should have thought twice
Because two hundred dollars
Wasn't worth
My unborn child's Life

The Messenger

Unlike any other messenger
I only bring the truth
Me without you are like trees without roots
It's like being in love with and angel
That's forbidden for anyone to touch
It's like a greed for acceptance
Sometimes it's too much
Nevertheless, we all take chances in
Our short life
Thinking of only ourselves, never thinking twice
Giving up nothing and who's to blame
Forgetting our fears
Only remembering our shame
Today is not forever, forever is not today
But when it comes, will you be willing to stay
I am only a messenger and nothing more
I have the key,
But will you open your door?

?Confused?

Confused am I, what did I see
All the joy, of wanting your needs
Kiss-n-tell is it true
These are the things that make me confused
Not knowing why and never how….
To answer questions that could be answered now
To-n-fro the wind will blow
Moving objects that's unknown
Taking away what I have found
Leaving nothing but a frown
I shall read and I shall look
For all the things confusion took
And when I find what I must seek
Only then can I sleep
Because as long as I'm without you
Only till then
Will I be confused?

Someday I Will Pray

Some days life isn't as fair as it may seem
I often give up on hope, but
Still try to fulfill my dreams
I teach myself and I'll try to learn
That tomorrow may be a different turn

A different turn in a direction that's far from far
A question in mind of who we are

Someday I'll pray, but nothing may change
A life of emptiness,
A life that's far from strange
A prayer for you, a prayer for me
A prayer that often ends while
Rising from my knees

Someday I'll pray
Someday I'll see that maybe
The lord is praying for me

If I

If I try a little harder
Or
If I climb a little higher

(Will you stay?)

If I run a little faster
Or
If I yell a little louder

(Will you stay?)

If I get down on one knee
Or
If I swam the seven seas

(Will you stay,

                Will you stay............?)

I See

I see your tears behind
Your hardened shell
A heart that beats louder
Than any southern bell

I see your torn feelings that
You try to hide
A broken heart that
Can't decide

I can hear the pity-pat
Of you wondering mind
Just look a little bit harder
Love isn't hard to find

I can see you looking forward
But your feet don't move
An uneducated heart that was
Once ruled by a fool

Open your eyes and try to see
What I see
Maybe then things will
Be better between
You and me

Shut Eyes

Opening shut eyes for the first time
Is hard in some cases
Realizing new faces and strange places
Looking through a closed window
And things appear the same
Walking out the door and for
The first time you feel strange
Watching the world go by
With your eyes shut
Missing everyday life, but
To you it wasn't much
Look, for there's a new world to see
Meadows, highways, rivers, and seas
Follow your heart
It may never lead you wrong,
But if it should just remember
You're not alone
Open your eyes and count your blessings
But only God can show you through
His eyes what you've been missing

Losing You

You don't have to bring the world to me
Just give me your word and let it be
Nothing I can give you will satisfy you,
Your sexual needs have already been met
Even though we haven't touched in a while
Believing that space is the only answer
(Well it's not)
I speak only when I must
Realizing that you can be trusted
Leaving us with space
Giving us the air we needed to breathe

If I

If I told you how I feel
Would you laugh at me?

If I told you what I have is free
Would you believe?

If I tried to hold you
Would you run?

If I tried to kiss you
Would you let me
Breathe into your lungs?

Death

When your heart can no longer breathe
And your air begins to leave,
Then you'll know that the time has come
Wasting time will become useful,
And feelings will become meaningless,
When trees begin to wither
And birds no longer sing
Then you'll know
When tomorrow doesn't matter
And the stars no longer gather
The faint sound of laughter
And you hear the calling of voices
In the hereafter
Then you'll know that life does matter

Friendship

Together forever, nothings as easy
And as clever as our friendship
From the first day to our last day
I hope that some of the time is
Spent with you

No kisses, nor hugs
Just smiles that gleam
Just you and me as funny
As it may seem

Don't worry if I'm not around
Even if sometimes I'm not on your mind
Just remember when we do meet
Everything will be fine

From the first child, to your last child
I hope everything's alright
Because our friendship is forever
Like day and night

For Mandy

The Angel

Would you believe if I told you
I saw an Angel
Not far from my window
As crazy as it may seem
I've never had an Angel
To enter my dreams
I was calm when she
Started walking towards me
Reaching our her hand as if
She was giving me something
And wouldn't you believe it
If it really was happening
She turned away looking back
Smiling
Her vision seem never ending
And slowly I went back to sleep
Crying because like you
She left me

When A Man Cries

How can a man find peace?
When his eyes won't let him forget
When he loses control of his self-respect
Bringing regrets and for one moment
Remembering once celibacy
Now it's only in his memories and
The bond he once had is left for
Future discovery
Who speaks now only in secrecy
With no honesty and a many of friends
He had deceived
A heart unknown to find his own destiny
Never to admit the things he has come to see
The many mistakes with no understandings
Is it love that makes him weak?
Or just his insecurity of forgiving himself
For stupidity of not caring
Barricading his mind from the truth

When a man cries

The Third Person

What voices do I hear while I sleep?
The sounds of whispering behind my back
While hearing footsteps creep
It doesn't take a genius to figure out
Who they are
When loneliness enters your mind
The third person isn't too far
Like a plague it only speaks to me when
No one's around
They talk of new beginnings and still I have not found
I'd rather ignore them, but their words are too clear
And if I push them away then no one else but me
Will remain here wondering
Who do I speak of without a name?
The third person only exist when my problems
I can't contain

Forbidden

One thought
    One mind
One word
    One time

I cannot bear to let this be
Something of impurity
Tonight is not tonight
Unless I can speak to thee
Of my inner thoughts of uncertainty

One voice
    One hand
One step
    One door

How can I ignore
Nothing may ever bring me relief
Trapped in between my speech
Too blind to see
My passion waiting to be free
Unforgiving to reality

One thought
    One mind
One heart
To beat as one, if for the last time

I Miss You

I miss you with every breath
I'll try to keep up with your fading
Steps of secret dreams
Which in my head are kept
I miss the things we once shared
Now no more and because of it
I'm scared,
They say a picture is worth a thousand words,
But nothing as meaningful as the ones I've heard,
I miss you
And everyday I wanted to cry
I miss you
Because you left without saying why

Unfaithful

I was too blind to see
The things you were doing to me,
You were stealing my heart
While I was asleep,
Returning before the morning break
With words untouched
And guilt written on your face
Your kisses no longer felt the same,
And your morning hugs
Somewhat strange,
The smell of sweet perfume
The odor of a different tune,
Your eyes the shade of
An unfamiliar color
The walk of a dishonest lover
Keeping my thoughts undercover
Remembering the things my father had done to my mother
The smile of a liar
And the passion of a cheat
Finding out that it was true
While talking in your sleep

BLINDED

I was blinded by your presence
And I could not believe
A million thoughts flash through my mind
A mutual bonding between you and me
I explored your physical form
And I dared not to touch
The wrong motions would leave your judgment stuck
My intentions wasn't harmful,
But yet are you ready.
I delivered my impression
But didn't know how far they would get me
So don't get me wrong
I'm only after your mind
Your secret thoughts I would soon know
In time words yet unspoken
Understanding that I'm not joking just hoping
That everything will be fine and
In my heart, I believe that your heart is true
Realizing that one day
I'll open my eyes and
Finally see me and you

My Mama

MAMA, I know at times you look a little sad
Wondering how you managed all those years
As a child I could never understand
You were vulnerable to the liking of a man
At one time your friend, but somehow
It fell apart at the end
And you smiled everyday, why did you stay
Instead you chose not to run away
From the truth
Throughout my youth I mentally abused you
The things I used to say and do
Now a regrettable fool, I do love you
Why did God let me do those things?
Now I know these memories won't let me sleep in peace
Oh my memories through my child eyes
Soon to be repeated
What comes around goes around
How my emotions fall to the ground
But you raised me, I was listening
How can I forget ?
You took care of me, when I was sick
My mama
My dear sweet mama
How I love thee

Me & money

It was unforgettable the first day that we met
Holding you in my hands, making a bond of respect
I often visualize things I would soon get
And whenever you weren't around it often made me sick
At times it made no sense
I would look for you day into the night
I thought you were my friend and
Your trust at times I had to fight
How could you leave me without saying a word?
Sometimes hearing rumors of you with someone else
At least that's what I heard
Did you forget about me taking everything that I had?
Leaving me in debt with society
And for that we are no longer friends
Me and money
I thought we'd last until
The end

Mistakes

I feel better now knowing that your
Heart now understands
The truth didn't set me free
And here is where I stand
Blinded by the fact that I'm still not considered
A man
I wish I could forget, you said that I can
We shared my worth, but only I shared
My love
I pushed you away frequently just because
My true identity was sealed within my heart
Unable to believe, for the temptation
I could not stop
Now I see how Noah felt while
Trapped on the Ark
It takes two to talk, but only one to react
For give me for my mistakes
Wishing you would take me back

The Shielded Truth

Covered eyes will not shield the visions
I seek
The countless hours, the week less weeks
I am here to stay
So I wait for tomorrow
I dream of acceptance
So there's no need for sorrow
I pray for the world
To acknowledge my name
I am a child of God
And not of fame
For I don't believe in wishes
I believe in miracles
Not reasons, but ambitions
He is the truth
Shielded no more
His truth is in his voice
How can one ignore?

Love Hung-over

At one time you were my ocean
And I was your distant land
Fate brought us together
One woman, one man
Love was the plan
What more to understand
Trying to block out the voices of communication
Instead of walking, I ran
Catching only the agony and pain
So many times, so many names and saying I'm sorry
Used to save me over and over again
Now to your ears it only sounds plain
And love at that time was not the blame
The feelings of guilt, the feelings of shame
Holding now the hand without a ring
Love has used me for the last time
Only to be left hung-over again

The Truth

Everything I've ever told you was the truth
Me without you are like trees without roots
No I'm not rich or even a millionaire,
But for your love I would take a thousand dares
To prove to you that I'm the one you need
You're like a rose in a garden of weeds
And I'm your champion honeybee
I've presented to you everything that
I have to give
My love, my comfort, my will to live
My heart beats for no one, but you
Will you take my offer and make my dreams come true?
I only bring you the truth and my hearts desire
No need for mistrust, because my heart's no liar
I'm willing and waiting and
I will do anything to prove that my love is
True

Footsteps

I've gotten used to you being with me
No matter where we're at,
Just the two of us together
My memories of you, I'll never forget
I remember hearing you trying to sneak up
Your uncontrollable laugh giving in
Watching you blush,
Now when I look around there's
Nothing to be found, not even your shadow
That used to follow me on the ground
Now that things are upside down
Turning my smile to a frown
I can't believe you used to walk on the
Very floors that I swept
I remember hearing your footsteps even when I slept
But slowly sometimes things come to pass
And with every fading footstep that
I thought would last
I'm glad of all the memories that
I kept, but most of all
I'll cherish hearing your last footsteps

Runaway

Runaway as fast as you can
I'll understand if it meant
Saving us then your decision
I'll have to trust
I'll meet you at the
End of the earth
I'll wait for you
For all that it's worth
And when you get there
Then we'll be together
Forever
And nothing can harm you
Just believe in me
Believe in the truth
Don't look back
Because yesterday's not there
So no need to be worried
Because I'm not scared to face you
Because my word is my shield
My truth is my sword
And your love is my will
Runaway with me until we reach
The end of time
At last I've found
Something that I can call mine
Run, runaway, because you're free
Run, runaway until you find me

A battle for love

I fought a many battles and
Few have I lost
But the fight for
your love has nearly cost
me everything
My life force is truly fading
Battle after battle waiting after waiting
I will never surrender nor give up hope
But his army is somewhat strong
But somehow I'll try to cope
Nearly waving a white flag
Thinking of compromising a truce
Knee deep in sorrow, but I'll find a better use
God's on my side and together we shall win
A battle for your love,
A battle to the bitter end

Fatherhood

Speak and you shall be heard
While looking in the mirror
Only to find a man-child
Thinking your voice is now not so loud
Following your emotions into a shadow less cloud
Where no one knows your name
And each facing day is the same
Puzzling your brain
Why should you share what you proclaimed?
What was yours no longer remains?
The thoughts you once had are
Borrowed over and over again
You're a father now,
So why do most complain
Once focused and for one minute insane
One night could ruin your outlooks
Bringing back your childhood books
And balancing your time is somehow shook
You're a father,
Be Proud of your child
Weather she or a he it's all good
So welcome yourself
To Fatherhood

The Last Day of Last Words

To each there own thoughts
And to each there own words
Yesterday I thought of what was
And what used to be
With questions unanswered
And feelings left open
Only left to remember that
Last chance
We're only here for a short while
And then we're gone
And what will we do and say
Until our last days,
Well I'll spend my last days
Searching for that one thing
At this time that means the most
Forgetting about lost words
And reaching for hope
My last words of choice
Will be this
Only to say hello and for you
To remember me for that
Because first words are only of forgetfulness
And the last words
You can always take back

For the sake of You

How do you tell an unborn child
That you won't be around some days?
All because I misbehaved,
Knowing me and his mom won't ever be married
How uncaring you must think
To choose between the one
You think that loves you the most
One choice both, we love then
Sometimes we hate its not too late
To reconcile our differences
For your sake for our mistakes
We must break for one minute
To get along and smile whenever
We're together just for the sake of you
We're willing to do

Just Believe

Tell me that you love me
For one last time,
Because I think I'm losing my mind,
I'm keeping and hoping your picture
Would turn to reality
Still believing in you and me,
Putting aside our differences so that we can again breathe
No need for greed, giving in to your needs,
If only you'll just believe and
Not deceive me,
I know that you're hurting and
Deserving someone who's loving and caring,
Who's love you do mind sharing,
What I've found buried beneath your frown
A beautiful smile that was bound
Then your voice sounds and you screamed
Waking me from my dream
Thinking did I make you believe me
Or was it all for nothing

Trading love

If you give me the sun
I will add it to my light
And if you give me day
Then I'll give you the night
But if life gives you pain
Then I'll give you my heart
And there's no need to explain
I'll trade anything for your love
Because there's nothing I wouldn't do for you
If you give me your word
Then I'll give you mine
An unconditional romance that's quite divine
If you give me your acknowledgeable love
Then I'll give you mine just because
Your innocence is all that I see
I will give all that I can
Until you achieve whatever
You're asking for
Hopefully it's me

Us

Each passing day takes us further away
Sending us in opposite directions
Pulling us apart
Loneliness possesses our mind
Making us walk straighter lines
Leaving nothing behind
Continuously going blind
And still love we can not find giving
Us feelings of not trying
With intentions of shattering our minds
Causing our ears to bust
Nobody cares because
Nobody knows but us

Born Again

Your voice is as soft
As a blooming flower
And your eyes sparkle
Like raindrops from an April shower,
Even though I may never touch you
I'm forever holding you
In my head,
Maybe you could tell me
What you're thinking
If I should ask
Or maybe you'd rather
Keep me guessing
In search of endless clues

Your touch is as gentle
As new born skin
And your smile is as friendly
As a bee's sting
So tell me your story
Is it true what they say?
That forever isn't forever
Until the last I see your face
Because through your eyes
I am born again

BETRAYED

I'll give up losing you
To preserve my happiness
Inside of me
Bringing new light from an utter darkness
Betrayed in my eyes and
Hated in my heart
A never ending battle of lust
And greed and your likeness I never needed
You cast your ugly shadow amongst
My shattered shame
And for my problems, you are to blame
A thousand moons cursed because
Of you
A forbidden love affair
Of a tenderhearted fool
Betrayed over and over again
At one time you were my friend
A remedy of hope was to be believed
An unsociably despised judgment
Of cruelty
I valued your trust
And to me it was to be an
Understanding only between us
Revolting an action echoing of being
Betrayed.., Betrayed…, Betrayed….,
Betrayed….., Betrayed……………,
Damned for eternity

Growing Young

Each day brings me closer
To the things I used to say
For most reasons I used to
Believe anything I heard
But now things are different
When you believe no more
How could it come to this?
So quickly
I'm a man now, but
I still have youthful memories
Of seeds that's now trees
I'm remembering running,
Whenever I scraped my knee,
Now I feel no need
Thinking what happened to my youthful years
Through my child's eyes
I can still see
Maybe I have a chance
To grow young again
Because I still believe

Judging me

Let no man judge me
For no man shares my
Personal problems,
How can he solve them?
If he never asks,
Judging me will only add
I am not a child anymore
So I shall be heard,
Even if no one is willing to listen,
All I need is one man to
Hear my words,
If one man hears my words
Then you'll see
My visions will spread
Like the widest sea
Judge me not
For here is where I stand
Say what you must,
While looking you in your eyes
And dare you to doubt me
As a man!

Familiar

At that time my heart
Didn't have a home,
Unknown to being faithful
But faithful to whom,
Stay with me
She constantly said,
My eyes never crossed
Her lips often leaving her mad,
For one day she may leave
Her love to be with me,
Forever trapped
In a world of jealousy,
Now my mind
Banded from the thoughts
Of a broken love
Mistrust and questions
With answers ending in
Just because,
She never knew
My real name,
Because after the first one
Many others before me came,
I wasn't the first
She couldn't contain
Remembering only what she became
My familiar, My love, My pain

RAINDROPS TO WATERFALLS

In the beginning, who knew of neglected thoughts
The long hours of thinking, the endless walks
The none responsive talks
Clouds forming within one's mind
Soon to be planted by guilt and misery
I will soon find the passion of mistakes
The love for hate, while my emotions continue to wait
I remember once feeling fine
A clear mind exposed to joy
Suddenly I have no need to reminisce anymore

Printed in the United States
53871LVS00002B/1-51